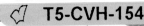

T5-CVH-154

THE UNFOLDING WORLD

AMAZING INSECTS

CONTENTS

THE FOLD-OUT PANORAMA

WHAT IS AN INSECT?

Insects have lived on Earth a long time. Fossilized ants, caught in amber millions of years ago, are found in rainforests.

Insects are the most successful life-form on our planet. There are more kinds of insects than all other types of animals and plants put together. More than half of all life on Earth belongs to the class *Insecta*. They have been here more than 360 million years, according to the fossil evidence, and first appeared long before the dinosaurs. Scientists have found more than a million different species of insects, and there may be another million more to find.

The millions of insects that are known are classified, that is, sorted out and named, using a system that was started almost 250 years ago by the Swedish naturalist Carl Linnaeus. This system uses Latin names so that it can be understood anywhere in the world.

Insects can live in extreme climates, such as the Arctic.

RIGHT *The common housefly is classified using the system invented by Linnaeus.*

PHYLUM

Similar classes make up a phylum. Insecta belong to the phylum Arthropoda.

CLASS

...milar orders make up a class. ...tera belong to the class Insecta.

ORDER

Similar families make up an order. Muscidae belong to the order Diptera.

FAMILY

Similar genuses make up a family. Musca belong to the family Muscidae.

GENUS

...milar species make up a genus. ...lies belong to the genus Musca.

The common housefly, Musca domestica, is one species of fly.

THE NAMING OF INSECTS

The species is the basic level. All members of a species are very much alike and can mate to produce fertile offspring. Species that are very much alike are grouped into a *genus;* several similar genuses make a *family;* similar families make up an *order;* similar orders are grouped into a *class*; and several classes make up a *phylum.*

3

BUGS THAT AREN'T INSECTS

MANY small creatures that we call "bugs" are not insects. Spiders, scorpions, daddy longlegs, ticks, and centipedes look a lot like insects, but if you inspect them closely you will see that they are different. They are related, as they all belong to the phylum *Arthropoda*. Arthropods are a group of animals with skeletons on the outside of their bodies. But they belong to different classes. Insects belong to the class *Insecta*. Other arthropods belong to different classes. Look on pages 2 and 3 to see the difference between a phylum and a class.

Many people are surprised to discover that crabs, crayfish, and shrimps are also related to insects. These animals are called crustaceans. They are also arthropods, but belong to the class *Crustacea*.

SPOT THE INSECTS

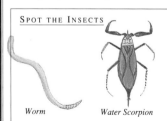

Worm   *Water Scorpion*

Water Beetle

WHICH BUG?

The easiest way to spot a non-insect is to count the legs and body parts. Compare the spider to the fly (LEFT), and you will see the difference. Spiders have two body segments and eight legs; the fly, being an insect, has six legs and three body parts.

Below are six "bugs". Only two are insects - but which are they? Here are some clues. Woodlice are related to crabs. Scorpions and centipedes have more than six legs. Worms have none. (ANSWERS BELOW).

SUCCESSFUL RELATIVES

Non-insect arthropods make up around eight per cent of all living plants and animals.

Answers:
Water Beetle; Water Scorpion

Scorpion

Woodlouse

Centipede

THE PARTS OF AN INSECT

Fore wing

Hind wing
Most adult winged
insects have two
pairs of wings

Every adult
insect has
three parts to its
body: *head, thorax,*
and *abdomen*. The
head carries eyes,
antennae, and
mouthparts.
Antennae are used
for smell and touch,
and some insects
hear with them. The
thorax, divided into
three segments,
carries legs and
wings.

*Cercus or
"tail"*

Abdomen

Ovipositor
(for laying eggs)

Hind legs
Insects have six legs,
one pair on each
segment of the thorax

Most insects have two kinds of eyes. The simple eye, called an *ocellus*, can do little more than sense light. *Compound eyes* can have thousands of lenses receiving lots of images.

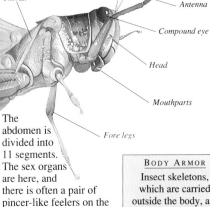

Ocellus

Compound eye

Thorax

Antenna

Compound eye

Head

Mouthparts

Fore legs

The abdomen is divided into 11 segments. The sex organs are here, and there is often a pair of pincer-like feelers on the last segment. Tiny openings called spiracles line the sides of the abdomen. These are for breathing.

BODY ARMOR

Insect skeletons, which are carried outside the body, are made from a light, tough, flexible material called *chitin*.

LIFE STAGES

MOST insects go through four stages in their lives. The change from one stage to the next is called *metamorphosis*. At each stage, the insect may look so different that you can't always tell that it is the same insect.

The first stage is the egg. From the egg hatches a small, worm–like animal. This is called the *larva*. The caterpillars of moths

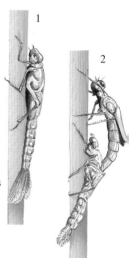

The damselfly nymph is born without wings (1). As it grows larger, it sheds its skin (2). Its wings gradually develop (3) and it keeps on growing until it becomes an adult (4).

and butterflies are *larvae*. The larva does only two things. It eats and it grows. When the larva reaches full size it becomes a *pupa*. Some *pupae* have shiny hard shells; others are silky, soft cocoons. At this stage, the insect seems not to move. But, inside the pupa, the insect's whole body is breaking down into a slime and rebuilding itself into the final stage. Weeks, sometimes months, later, the adult insect emerges. The adult soon lays eggs to start the whole process again.

3

4

THE SIMPLE LIFE

Some insects hatch from the egg looking like smaller versions of the adult, with some parts missing, such as wings. These junior insects are called *nymphs*. As they grow, the missing parts develop. This process is called *simple* or *incomplete* metamorphosis.

ADAPTATIONS

The grasshopper has mouthparts designed for biting and chewing.

INSECTS live in so many different environments that almost every part of their bodies has evolved and become specially adapted for their survival.

This is very easy to see in the mouthparts. Most insects have an upper lip (called the *labrum*), a lower lip (*labium*), jaws (*mandibles*) and two smaller hanging jaws (*maxillae*).

From these basics, the mouthparts of each insect have adapted to deal with what that insect eats and how it gets to its food supply.

Different designs include mouths for biting and chewing (like grasshoppers), piercing and sucking (like weevils), lacerating and sucking (like horseflies), chewing and lapping (like sawflies), sucking and lapping (like houseflies), and siphoning (like butterflies). Flies live on a liquid diet, so their mouthparts are made to suck or lap up their food.

The leafhopper has mouthparts designed for sucki

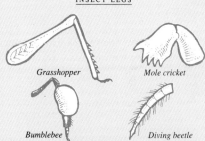

INSECT LEGS

Grasshopper

Mole cricket

Bumblebee

Diving beetle

The legs of an insect also tell you a lot about how it survives. Grasshoppers' hind legs are thick and strong, giving the insect its jumping ability. Bumblebees have pollen-carrying sacs on their hind legs. Mole crickets spend most of their lives tunneling through the soil. They have flat, front legs that look like spades. Diving beetles have fringes of hair on their legs to help them push through the water.

Wings too have developed in many different ways. Most butterflies have large, flat wings for slow but long flight. Dragonflies have long, light, quick-moving wings for fast, short flight. Beetles have stubby, light, hind wings that "shoot" the insect quickly over short distances.

PROTECTIVE COLORING

COLOR is another way that insects use to survive. Some insects blend into their surroundings, but many do not hide at all. Their colors make them stand out.

One of these is the Monarch butterfly. Its wings are bright orange, outlined with black. This color pattern calls attention to the butterfly and warns off other animals which might try and eat the monarch. It is a useful warning, because the monarch butterfly caterpillar feeds on milkweed leaves, which are poisonous to birds.

Another is the bright pink nymph (young insect) of the stink bug that lives in the Borneo rainforest. Its color clearly warns that it protects itself with a smelly, poisonous fluid.

The Malaysian hawk moth caterpillar turns itself into a small snake when attacked. Its front segments stretch, revealing a huge pair of false eyes, and it sways on its twig in a menacing manner.

The bright color of this member of the shieldbug family warns hunters that it is a "stinkbomb". When attacked, it produces a foul smell from the stink glands on the side of its thorax.

Other insects have similar bright colors but are not poisonous. They rely on looking like poisonous species for their protection. This is called *mimicry*. Several butterfly species mimic the monarch butterfly. One of the most common is the viceroy butterfly, which has the same colors and pattern, but is harmless. Hoverflies, wasp beetles, beeflies, and hornet moths are also harmless. They have no stings, but copy the black and yellow warning colors of bees and wasps.

Bright colors are also found on certain parts of some insects. Some moths have bright, flashy hind wings that are only seen when the insect flies away. This sudden show of color startles attackers.

Big, bright eyespots that have nothing to do with seeing work the same way. They confuse predators, by making them think they are seeing a much larger animal, or an animal pointing in the opposite direction.

FLYING COLORS

More bright colors are found on more insects than any other group of animals.

CAMOUFLAGE

WHILE some insects show off their colors, others use bright color to hide from attack by blending into their backgrounds. This is called camouflage. Many grasshoppers are patterned in patches of light and dark, just like the camouflage pattern on some military uniforms. This breaks up their shape and makes it difficult for a predator to see their outline properly.

Other insects have taken this even further. Their entire bodies have adapted to help them hide from predators. Walkingsticks look exactly like sticks or twigs. Many leafhoppers look like thorns. The leaf butterfly resembles a dead leaf hanging on the stalk of a plant. Some moths look like patches of tree bark.

The glass swallowtail butterfly from Indonesia lives in a rainforest. Its bright colors help it blend with the trees and flowers.

The bush cricket, shown in the close-up (LEFT), can be very hard to spot when it sits still on a tree branch.

bush cricket

Flattid bugs, which look like moths, cluster together on a plant stem to look like flowers. Some butterfly caterpillars can pass for bird droppings. It is very difficult for a predator to spot these insects on the forest floor, in a path of weeds, or along the side of a tree trunk or weed stem. Not all camouflage is for defense. It is also used by insects that lurk in ambush for their prey. For example, the bright pink orchid mantis stands out obviously against green leaves, but spends most of its time among flowers that hide it. It waits among the blossoms until some unsuspecting insect stops for nectar, and then grabs it.

> FAMILY
> RESEMBLANCE
>
> Thorn moths look like dried leaves and their caterpillars look like twigs.

INSECT HUNTERS

THERE are many hunters in the insect kingdom, and they have many different ways to find and capture their prey. The assassin bug stabs its prey with its long, sharp beak, or proboscis, and injects venom. After the prey is dead, the assassin bug uses the same proboscis to suck out the body juices.

Dragonflies hunt while flying. Holding their legs in a "basket" position under their bodies, the dragonflies scoop up small flying insects. Water bugs grab and hold their prey to inject them with venom.

Most species of wasp paralyze their prey by stinging. Then they store it alive in cells ready for the wasp larvae to feed on later.

Assassin bugs are great hunters. They feed on insects and spiders. This one is sucking the body juices of a millipede.

The ant lion digs a small pit in the sand and buries itself in it, leaving only its jaws showing. Then it waits for ants and other small insects to slide down the sides.

Some insects look like mighty hunters, but actually eat nothing but plant material. Stag beetles belong to this harmless group. They look very fierce and they can give you a nasty pinch with their large, antler-like jaws, but they don't use those jaws for hunting.

Other insects don't look much like hunters, but spend at least part of their lives killing and eating other insects. For example, the harvester is a gossamer–winged butterfly whose caterpillar eats all the aphids it can find.

THE STING

Only female bees and wasps have stings. Worker bees die when they sting, as the sting is ripped out of the abdomen, but queen bees and all wasps can sting repeatedly.

GOOD BUGS

Ladybug

M OST of the insects that we call "good" are the hunters that kill the insects that we call "bad" because they damage gardens and crops. Good bugs come in a variety of species. Wasps are not usually thought to be friendly, but they are very useful. Many wasps eat flies, aphids, and weevils.

Dung beetle

The praying mantis looks like a fierce hunter and it is. The little ladybug doesn't look like it could hurt anything; but both of them eat large numbers of aphids, which are very bad insects to the gardener and the farmer.

Good bugs need not be hunters. Dung beetles lay eggs in the dung of cattle, sheep, and horses. The larvae break up and eat the dung, which would otherwise smother the ground.

The praying mantis feeds on aphids by picking them up between its front legs.

Praying mantis

BAD BUGS

Mosquito

IT'S IMPORTANT to remember that no insect is really "good" or "bad". Insects do what they will, and if we don't like it we call the insect "bad". In reality, less than one percent of all insects damage crops, but this costs millions of dollars. "Bad" bugs include various species of aphids, thrips, beetles, weevils, chafers and locusts. They attack all kinds of food crops: grains, vegetables, and fruit. The boll weevil attacks cotton plants.

Apple sawfly

Science has given us many chemicals to deal with insect problems, but recently we've learned that some of these also damage our environment and other species they were never intended for. A safer way to combat insect pests is to encourage the "good" bugs.

Colorado beetle

> ### INSECT VILLAINS
> Colorado beetles destroy potato crops. Apple sawflies ruin apple harvests. Mosquitoes spread disease, particularly malaria, among humans.

THE BEEHIVE

MOST insects spend almost their entire lives alone. However, some species of ants, bees, wasps, and termites live in orderly, complex societies.

The honeybee has the most advanced society of any insect. Within the hive, the bees are organized into different levels, called *castes*. There is one queen,

All the work in the hive is done by worker bees, females who cannot lay eggs. Worker bees live for about six weeks. They begin life as cleaners. After a few days they become nurses, feeding the larvae and the queen with royal jelly produced from special glands in their mouths. After 10 days, they begin making wax to build and mend the hive. Next, they store pollen and nectar and stand guard at the hive entrance. Their last job is to go out foraging among the flowers.

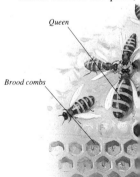

Queen

Brood combs

who lays all the eggs; a few male drones who do nothing except mate with the queen; and hundreds of worker bees. They build the hive and keep it clean. They gather pollen and nectar and turn it into honey to feed the larvae. Armed with stings, they defend the hive. This work plan is programmed into them from the day they emerged as adults.

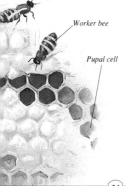

Worker bee

Pupal cell

The hive is built by the worker bees, using wax produced by their own bodies. There is a chamber for the huge queen bee and individual cells for her to lay eggs in. These are grouped together in brood combs. Other cells are used to store pollen and honey.

ANT COLONIES AND TERMITE MOUNDS

JUST LIKE honeybees, ant society includes males, queens, and workers. The system works a lot like the bees' hive, but there are great differences in how ant colonies survive. Some are predators, capturing and killing other insects for their food. Some are vegetarian, with the workers cutting off bits of plant leaves and feeding the colony. Others are farmers, tending "herds" of aphids for their honey-dew. And others, called army ants, move the entire colony over great distances raiding everything they come across.

Termite mounds are topped by tall towers or chimneys. These funnel fresh air down to the colony below. Seven million termites may live in one colony.

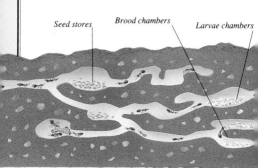

Seed stores

Brood chambers

Larvae chambers

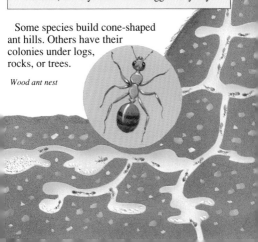

LIFE IN THE MOUND

The champion home-builders in the insect world are the African mound-building termites. Using their own saliva with soil and sand, they build steadily for years. The pointed mounds rise slowly but may reach up to 18 feet.

Although termites have a society like the ants, they actually belong to the cockroach family. Like the bees and the ants, the termites' society revolves around the queen. She is much larger than the other termites, and lays thousand of eggs every day.

Some species build cone-shaped ant hills. Others have their colonies under logs, rocks, or trees.

Wood ant nest

INSECTS IN WINTER

IN the cool regions of the world, insects react to the approaching cold of late fall and winter in various ways. You've probably noticed that there are very few insects to be seen in your backyard in winter.

The cockchafer larva hibernates underground.

But if you look closely along the sides of tree trunks and twigs, along weed stems, and under logs or rocks you will find that most of the common insects are still there. They're just in a different form than they were in summer.

Now, it's their eggs and pupae that you'll find.

One of the strangest winter forms is the egg-case of the bagworm which looks exactly like a pine-cone hanging from a twig.

Another interesting egg-case is that of the praying mantis. It is a light brown clump of material that feels like styrofoam when you touch it gently.

Many beetles, weevils, and fireflies will hibernate in their adult forms. They go to sleep all through the winter. You can find them along the outside walls of your home and inside rotting logs. Most butterflies hibernate as larvae or pupae, but others fly south in the winter.

EGGS AND PUPAE

The bagworm spends winter in an egg-case that looks like a pine-cone shaped bundle of tiny sticks and bits of leaves.

egg case

pupa

Painted lady and monarch butterflies fly hundreds of thousands of miles south to escape the cold. They spend the winter there, coming back to the north with the spring.

INSECT ORDERS

INSECTS are divided into 29 orders. Look on pages 2 and 3 to see more about orders. The insects in each order look rather like each other or behave in the same way. When you find or observe an insect, note down its most noticeable characteristics: size, number of legs, wings, mouthpart design, whether there is a tail. If you look at the descriptions and diagrams given here, you will be able to work out which order it could belong to. Once you know that, you'll be able to discover some of its closest relatives.

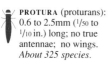

COLLEMBOLLA (springtails): less than 5mm ($1/5$ in.) long; no tails; mid-sized to long antennae; abdomen for jumping; no wings. *About 6,000 species.*

THYSANURA (thysanurans): 3 to 30mm ($1/8$ to $1 1/5$ in.) long; three tails; long antennae; abdomen not for jumping; no wings. *About 580 species.*

PROTURA (proturans): 0.6 to 2.5mm ($1/50$ to $1/10$ in.) long; no true antennae; no wings. *About 325 species.*

DIPLURA (diplurans): 2 to 50mm ($1/12$ to 2 in.) long; long tail or forceps; thick antennae; short legs; no wings. *About 660 species.*

EPHEMEROPTERA

(mayflies): 1 to 30mm ($1/25$ to $1^1/5$ in.) long; two or three long curving tails; veined membrane wings as adults. *About 2,000 species.*

ODONATA

(dragonflies and damselflies): 20 to 190mm ($4/5$ to $7^3/5$ in.) long; no tail; very short antennae; wings out at sides or closed over abdomen; veined membrane wings as adult. *About 4,950 species.*

PLECOPTERA

(stoneflies): 1 to 30mm ($1/25$ to $1^1/5$ in.) long; no tail or very short tail; broad, flat body; widely separated legs; veined membrane wings as adult. *About 1,550 species.*

GRYLLOBLATTODEA

(rockcrawlers): 14 to 30mm ($2/3$ to $1^1/5$ in.) long; short tail; long legs; large head; long antennae; no wings. *About 20 species.*

ORTHOPTERA

(grasshopppers, crickets, katydids): mostly 10 to 50mm ($2/5$ to 2 in.) long; enlarged hind legs for jumping; hind wings fold under front wings; front wings are thicker; always with wings as adults; chewing mouthparts. *About 12,500 species.*

PHASMIDA

(walkingsticks): 10 to 300mm ($2/5$ to 12 in.) long, but most are 70mm (3 in.) or less; long body; long thin legs; hind wings fold under front wings; no wings at some stages. *About 2,000 species.*

DICTYOPTERA (mantids and cockroaches) : 10 to 165mm (²/5 to 6¹/5 in.) long; broad, flattened body; in mantids, front legs enlarged to grab prey; in cockroaches, all legs thin; hind wings fold under front wings; front wings thicker; always with wings as adults.
About 5,500 species.

ISOPTERA (termites): 3 to 10mm (¹/8 to ²/5 in.) long; broad, flattened body, mostly abdomen; black or yellow head; white body; no wings at some stages.
About 1,900 species.

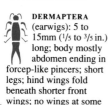

DERMAPTERA (earwigs): 5 to 15mm (¹/5 to ³/5 in.) long; body mostly abdomen ending in forcep-like pincers; short legs; hind wings fold beneath shorter front wings; no wings at some stages, but always wings as adult.
About 1,100 species.

EMBIOPTERA (webspinners): 4 to 22mm (¹/6 to 1 in.) long, but most are 7mm (¹/3 in.) or less; enlarged first segment of front legs; two pairs of long, thin wings (only in adult male).
About 150 species.

ZORAPTERA (zorapterans): 2 to 3mm (¹/12 to ¹/8 in.) long; rounded body; small legs; small antennae; two pairs of veined membrane wings.
About 25 species.

PSOCOPTERA (barklice and booklice): 1.5 to 5mm (³/50 to ¹/5 in.) long; long antennae; enlarged hind legs; no wings; no abdominal tails or forceps.
About 1,100 species.

MALLOPHAGA (chewing lice): 0.5 to 6mm ($1/50$ to $1/4$ in.) long; flat body; very short antennae; short legs; no wings; chewing mouthparts; always on animals or their nests. *About 2,675 species.*

ANOPLURA (lice): 0.4 to 5mm ($1/50$ to $1/5$ in.) long; flat but rounded body; very short antennae; short legs; no wings; sucking mouthparts; always on animals or man. *About 250 species.*

THYSANOPTERA (thrips): 0.4 to 14mm ($1/50$ to $3/5$ in.) long; large abdomen; two pairs of fringed wings; always have wings as adult. *About 4,000 species.*

HEMIPTERA (true bugs): 0.5 to 55mm ($1/50$ to $2^{1}/5$ in.) long; broad, rounded body; when closed, wings leave triangle at center of body; always have membrane wings as adult; sucking mouthparts. *About 23,000 species.*

HOMOPTERA (cicadas, aphids, leafhoppers): 1 to 90mm ($1/25$ to $3^{3}/8$ in.) long, but most are 55mm ($2^{1}/5$ in.) or less; broad, stocky body; very small antennae; front legs arched forwards strongly; always with wings as adult; both pairs of wings held over abdomen at rest; hind wings do not fold. *About 32,000 species.*

NEUROPTERA (neuropterans): 5 to 160mm ($1/5$ to $6^{3}/5$ in.) long; short abdomen without tails; mid-sized to long antennae; always with veined membrane wings as adult; wings are held over abdomen. *About 4,600 species.*

COLEOPTERA (beetles, weevils): 0.025 to 150mm ($1/1000$ to 6 in.) long, but most are 2 to 20mm ($1/10$ to $4/5$ in.); rounded, stout body, often armored; short antennae; moderately long legs; always with wings as adults; hind wings are folded beneath the short front wings; chewing mouthparts. *About 290,000 species.*

MECOPTERA (scorpionflies): 3 to 30mm ($1/8$ to $1^1/5$ in.) long, but most are 10 to 12mm ($1/2$ to $5/8$ in.); long head with snout; elongated legs; no wings; no tail or forceps. *About 350 species.*

 TRICHOPTERA (caddisflies): 1.5 to 40mm ($3/50$ to $13/5$ in.) long, but most are 8 to 20mm ($1/3$ to $4/5$ in.) long; long, slender body; large veined membrane wings, covered with fine hairs; always with wings as adult; very long, thin antennae curving forward; usually found near water. *About 180,000 species.*

 LEPIDOPTERA (butterflies, skippers, moths): 2 to 150mm ($1/12$ to 6 in.) long, but most are 5 to 80mm ($1/5$ to $3^1/5$ in.); long, thin bodies, covered with scales; large wings held over body; always with wings as adult. *About 180,000 species.*

HYMENOPTERA (bees, wasps, ants): 0.2 to 115mm ($^1/_{100}$ to $4^3/_5$ in.) long; highly segmented body; abdomen usually attached to thorax by narrow band; veined membrane wings without scales or hairs; often with stingers.
About 103,000 species.

 DIPTERA (flies): 0.5 to 75mm ($^1/_{50}$ to 3 in.) long, but most are less than 50mm (2 in.); rounded body; only one pair of veined membrane wings; often very large eyes; small antennae; long legs; no tail or forceps.
About 85,000 species.

 SIPHONOPTERA (fleas): 1 to 5mm ($^1/_{25}$ to $^1/_5$ in.) long; tight, rounded body; hind legs enlarged for jumping; no wings.
About 1,370 species.

OBSERVING INSECTS

In the past, books like this would talk about how you could collect insects and keep them. Today, a better idea is to observe them alive, making notes and sketches. Always get as close to the insect as you can. Use a magnifying glass if the insect is tiny or you want to see more detail. Note the time of day, the weather conditions, where you found it, what it was doing, and what species you think it is. After a summer of observation you will have made your own guide to the insects in your backyard.

RAISING A BUTTERFLY

Make your own "observatory" so you can look at the way insects develop without hurting them.

In the weeds near your home, look for a butterfly caterpillar. Capture it by holding one of your hands under the leaf it's on and snapping a plastic glass over the insect with your other hand. Then follow the directions below.

1

2

3

Find a butterfly caterpillar on a leaf. Place it in a large glass jar, on its leaf, adding plenty of similar leaves for food. Make sure the jar lid has plenty of small holes.

Remove stalks and add fresh leaves every day until the caterpillar turns into a chrysalis (usually a few weeks). Check the chrysalis twice a day.

Eventually you will see the adult butterfly breaking through. Allow the butterfly to stretch its wings for a few hours. Then release it where you collected the caterpillar.

A RUNNING PRESS / QUARTO BOOK

Joint copyright © 1993 Running Press / Quarto Publishing plc
Printed in China. All rights reserved under the Pan-American
and International Copyright Conventions.

Canadian representatives:
General Publishing Co., Ltd.,
30 Lesmill Road, Don Mills, Ontario M3B 2T6.

9 8 7 6 5 4 3 2 1

Digit on the right indicates the number of this printing.

Library of Congress
Cataloging-in-Publication Number 92-50789

ISBN 1-56138-226-4

Designed by PETER BRIDGEWATER
Edited by VIV CROOT
Illustrated by TONY MASERO

This book may be ordered by mail from the publisher.
Please add $2.50 for postage and handling.
But try your bookstore first!

RUNNING PRESS BOOK PUBLISHERS
125 South Twenty-second Street
Philadelphia, Pennsylvania 19103

THE FOLD-OUT PANORAMA

The fold-out panoramic chart opposite shows a selection of insects in their various habitats throughout the world: deserts, broad-leaved woodlands, polar regions, grasslands, rainforests, mountains, meadows, the seaside, and towns and cities. The insects illustrated have been chosen to represent as many of the insect orders as possible, and to show how successfully insects can adapt to life in every part of the world.

*mantis
rld's
s. It
cies

ters*

Springtails are the
world's most
primitive insects.
They live in grass,
soil, logs, leaf litter,
sand, and the edges
of rock pools.

Mosquitoes
are not only
tropical
insects. Many live near
the stagnant water pools that
are left behind when the tundra
snow melts.

**IN THE ARCTIC, ANTARCTIC,
AND TUNDRA REGIONS,
THERE ARE MILLIONS OF
INSECTS BUT NOT MANY
DIFFERENT SPECIES.**

*Australian stink bug nymphs
look like bright pink leaves.
Glands in the nymph's
abdomen produce foul-
smelling, bad-tasting liquid
drive away attackers.*

Caddis flies live aro
pools of the Arctic tun
Their larvae live
under water, where
they make nets to
catch food.

Warble
flies live in the
Arctic regions as parasites
on the caribou deer. They
lay eggs in the animal's
hair and the larvae burrow
into its skin.

Midges live all over the
world, including Arctic regions.
Only the females bite and suck blood.

◄ Mayflies live only a few hours. As adults, they have no mouths and cannot eat.

Scorpionflies are not true flies. They have four wings instead of two. ▼

Honeybees live a highly organized social life. Foraging honeybees are workers in the last stages of their short, six-week lives. ►

Whirligig beetles live in water. They "swim" by twisting their bodies round very fast.

Stoneflies live and bree near water. They eat wa insects and pla

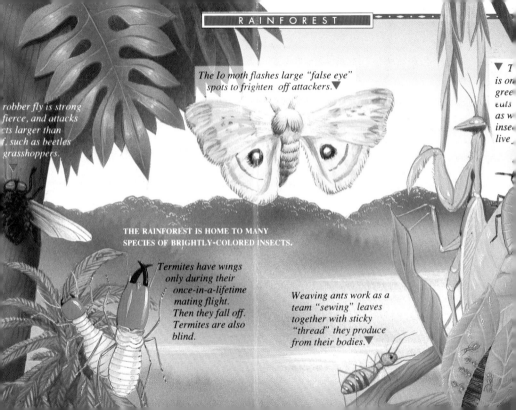

The Io moth flashes large "false eye"
spots to frighten off attackers.▼

robber fly is strong
fierce, and attacks
cts larger than
f, such as beetles
grasshoppers.

▼ *T*
is or
gree
euls
as w
inse
live.

THE RAINFOREST IS HOME TO MANY
SPECIES OF BRIGHTLY-COLORED INSECTS.

Termites have wings
only during their
once-in-a-lifetime
mating flight.
Then they fall off.
Termites are also
blind.

Weaving ants work as a
team "sewing" leaves
together with sticky
"thread" they produce
from their bodies.▼

**STREAMS, MOUNTAINS, AND MEADOWS ARE
HOME TO AQUATIC INSECTS AND
BEAUTIFUL BUTTERFLIES.**

*Horseflies are large
insects that sting
horses. Their
other name
is gadfly.* ▶

▲ *Cricket wasps live
around the sand
dunes of the coast.*

**INSECTS OF THE COASTAL REGION
MOSTLY LIVE AMONG SAND DUNES OR
ON CHALKY CLIFF TOPS.**

*...re a
...e to
...s and
...ners.
...stroy
...od
...s is an*

INSE
HAV
LIFE
WAR

▲ *The apollo butterfly is one of the many
beautiful species that live in the alpine region.*

*The hoverfly wears the
wasp's aggressive
black and yellow
colors, but is
harmless itself.* ▶

▶

*b...
e...
g...
a...*